the called *&* gifted *workshop*

Introduction

Participants in the *Called & Gifted Workshop* have found helpful various resources that enable them to discern and understand their gifts in the larger context of Church teaching and experience. The second edition of *Catholic Spiritual Gifts Resource Guide* in your hands is a revised and updated version of the resource sheets that were available only to those taking the workshop.

The first section contains references to primary sources for Church teaching on charisms in general and on the lay office. The remainder of the *Guide* is dedicated to specific resources to help someone explore more deeply the twenty-four charisms covered in the *Catholic Spiritual Gifts Inventory*. It includes:

- The charisms, listed in alphabetical order, along with a brief definition.

- A list of passages relevant to the exercise of each charism from both Scripture and the *Catechism of the Catholic Church*. Although not exhaustive, the references do include direct references to the charism, descriptions of it in action, or passages that present a brief background of Biblical and Church teaching helpful for anyone seeking to exercise the charism effectively as a Catholic disciple of Jesus Christ. The title *Catechism of the Catholic Church* is abbreviated as *CCC* throughout the *Resource Guide*.

- A list of recommended books (most of them currently in print) that deal in general with the exercise of the charism from a Christian perspective.

- A list of possible ways in which the charism might be exercised both within the parish setting and in our daily lives outside the parish.

- A list of "patron saints" for each charism. These great women and men of God have *not* been declared by the Church to be patrons of these charisms. I have named them honorary "patrons" because there is historical evidence that each of them exercised the charism in question during their lifetime.

The list of partons is by no means exhaustive and continues to grow. Most of them have been formally declared saints or blessed by the Church, but a few have not, although their causes may be underway. All were recognized in their lifetimes as exemplary Christians whose lives were remarkably creative and fruitful for the Kingdom of God. Just as during the Feast of All Saints we honor the great multitude of saints in heaven who have not been canonized, so in this *Guide* have I felt free to encourage those discerning a particular gift to take as a patron and model a great Christian who has been mightily used of God in that same area in the past.

Finally, I want to mention that many excellent resources are available on the Internet. Please see our website and visit our "links" pages for more information (www.siena.org).

Sherry Weddell
February 2003

Sources of Catholic teaching on charisms

■ Primary scriptural passages

Luke 24: 49
Acts
I Corinthians 12–14
Hebrews 2:4
II Timothy 1:6–7

John 14:12; 20:21-22
Romans 12
Ephesians 4
I Timothy 4:14

■ Patristic and medieval writers

Didache 10, 11

Ignatius of Antioch:
  Introduction to Smyrnians
  To Polycarp 2, 2
  To Philadelphians 7, 1, 2

Hermas, *The Shepherd* "Mandates" 11, 1–3, 9, 12

Justin Martyr, *Dialogue with Trypho* 30, 31, 82, 88

Ireneus, *Against the Heresies* 1, 13, 4; 2, 32, 4; 3, 11, 9; 3, 24, 1; 4, 26, 5; 5, 6, 1; 5, 16, 7; 5, 17, 4

Tertullian, *On Baptism* 20

the **called** *&* **gifted** *workshop*

The Catholic Spiritual Gifts Resource Guide
by Sherry Weddell

Table of Contents

Introduction 3

Sources of Catholic teaching on charisms 4

Sources of Catholic teaching
on the role and office of the laity 7

Resource guide for the charisms 9

Appendix 74

the **called** *&* **gifted** *workshop*

Copyright © 2003 by Sherry Weddell

Second edition

All rights reserved. No part of this book may be reproduced in any form or by any means without permission from the author, except for brief passages for the sake of criticism or review.

Printed in the United States of America

The Siena Institute Press
PO Box 26492
Colorado Springs, Colorado 80936

(719) 219-0056

www.siena.org

ISBN: 1-891996-02-9

Origen:

> *On John* 2, 10, 73–77; 6, 33; 8, 48
> *On First Principles*, Preface 2–3; 1, 3, 8; 2, 7, 3; 2, 10, 7
> *Against Celsus* 1, 44; 3, 46
> *Homilies on Jeremiah* 2, 3; 8, 5, 25
> *Homilies on Exodus* 4, 4–5
> *Commentary on the Psalms* 64, 11

Eusebius, *Ecclesiastical History* 3, 31, 4–5; 3, 37, 1; 4, 18, 8; 5, 1, 49; 5, 3, 4; 5, 7, 2–6; 5, 16, 8; 5, 17, 4; 8, 10, 3

Hilary of Poitiers:

> *On Matthew* 15, 10
> *On the Trinity* 1, 38; 2, 34–35, 8, 29–35
> *Tract on the Psalms* 63, 2–3; 64, 6; 64, 14–15

Cyril of Jerusalem, *Catechetical Lectures* 16, 17

Basil the Great, *On the Holy Spirit* 9, 23; 26, 61; 29, 73

Gregory Nazianzus, *Fifth Theological Discourse* 28, 29

Apostolic Constitutions 3, 16–18; 7, 22, 39–45; 8, 1, 21; 8, 23, 2–3; 8, 26, 2

John Chrysostom:

> *On I Corinthians* 29, 32, 35–36
> *On Romans* 14

Thomas Aquinas, *Summa Theologiae* I–II, 111, 4; I–II, 111, 5; I–II, 111, 1; I–II, 68, 5 ad 1; I–II, 66, 2 ad 1; II–II, 171–178

■ Documents of the Second Vatican Council that reference charisms

Dogmatic Constitution on the Church (*Lumen Gentium*), sections 4, 7, 12, 25, 30, 50

Decree on the Apostolate of the Laity (*Apostolicam Actuositatem*), sections 3, 30

Decree on the Ministry and Life of Priests (*Presbyterorum Ordinis*), section 9

Decree on the Church's Missionary Activity (*Ad Gentes*), sections 4, 23, 28

the **called** *&* **gifted** *workshop*

■ Papal Documents that reference charisms

On Evangelization in the Modern World (*Evangelii Nuntiandi*) 49, 73-74

Redeemer of Man (*Redemptor Hominis*) 19, 27, 74

The Vocation and Mission of the Lay Faithful in the Church and in the World (*Christifideles Laici*) 20-25, 27, 31-32, 45, 55, 64

The Gospel of Life (*Evangelium Vitae*) 78

Mission of the Redeemer (*Redemptoris Missio*) 18, 23, 66

Role of the Christian Family in the Modern World (*Familiaris Consortio*) 5, 16

Letter to Families 16

On the Dignity and Vocation of Women (*Mulieris Dignitatem*) 21, 27, 31

Letter to Women 11

Catechesis in Our Time (*Catechesi Tradendae*) 72

Consecrated Life (*Vita Consecrata*) 1-5, 9-12, 16-19, 25, 27, 30-31, 36-37, 42, 45-49, 53-68, 70-83, 93-99, 101-102, 109

I Will Give You Shepherds (*Pastores Dabo Vobis*) 16-18, 26, 29, 31, 38, 40-41, 44, 50, 59, 66, 74

On the Coming of the Third Millenium (*Tertio Millennio Adveniente*) 23, 38, 44, 46-47

■ Sections of the *Catechism of the Catholic Church* that reference specifically the charisms

94, 688, 798–801, 809, 890, 910, 924, 951, 1175, 1506-1508, 2003-2004, 2024, 2035, 2684

■ Recommended books

The Holy Spirit, Lord and Giver of Life (The official catechetical text in preparation for the Jubilee.), Crossroads Publishing Company.

Christian Initiation and Baptism in the Holy Spirit: Evidence from the First Eight Centuries, Killian McDonnell and George T. Montague. Michael Glazier.

the **called** *&* **gifted** *workshop*

Sources of Catholic teaching on the role and mission of laity

■ **Documents of the Second Vatican Council**

Dogmatic Constitution on the Church (*Lumen Gentium*) 9-17, 27-28, 30-42

Decree on the Apostolate of the Laity (*Apostolicam Actuositatem*)

Pastoral Constitution on the Church in the Modern World (*Gaudium et Spes*)

Decree on the Bishop's Pastoral Office in the Church (*Christus Dominus*), sections 6, 15, 17, 22, 27, 30

Decree on Priestly Formation (*Optatam Totius*), sections 6, 11, 20

Decree on the Ministry and Life of Priests (*Presbyterorum Ordinis*), sections 2, 9, 21

Decree on the Church's Missionary Activity (*Ad Gentes*), sections 1, 11-12, 15, 17, 20-21, 23, 26, 29, 30, 36, 41

■ **Documents of Pope John Paul II referencing aspects of the lay office**

On Christ's work of redemption:
Redeemer of Man (*Redemptor Hominis*)

On the Holy Spirit:
Lord and Giver of Life (*Dominum et Vivificantem*)

On the laity:
The Vocation and Mission of the Lay Faithful in the Church and in the World (*Christifideles Laici*)

On the Church's mission of evangelism:
On the Permanent Validity of the Church's Missionary Mandate (*Redemptoris Missio*)
On the Unicity and Salvific Universality of Jesus Christ and the Church (*Dominus Iesus*)

On Catholic social teaching and the renewal of the temporal order:
    On Human Work (*Laborem Exercens*)
    The Splendor of Truth (*Veritatis Splendor*)
    Faith and Reason (*Fides et Ratio*)
    The Gospel of Life (*Evangelium Vitae*)
    On the Hundredth Anniversary of Rerum Novarum
        (*Centisimus Annus*)
    On the Coming of the Third Millenium (*Tertio Millenio Adveniente*)

On the mission of women:
    On the Dignity and Vocation of Women (*Mulieris Dignitatem*)
    Letter to Women (on the eve of the Fourth World Conference on Women held in 1995 in Beijing)

On family life:
    On the Family (*Familiaris Consortio*)
    Letter to Families

■ **Sections of the *Catechism* that reference specifically the identity and mission of the laity:**

CCC: 782-786, 794-795, 863-865, 871-873, 897-913, 928-929, 934, 940-943, 1141-1144, 1174-1178, 1213-1321, 1533-1535, 1546, 1591, 1601-1664, 1669, 1877-1948, 1934-1935, 2225-2231, 2442

■ **Recommended books**

To Hunt, to Shoot, to Entertain: Clericalism and the Catholic Laity, Russell Shaw. Ignatius Press.

The Parish: Mission of Maintenance, Michael Sweeney, OP and Sherry Weddell. Siena Institute Press.

Making Disciples, Equipping Apostles: the Parish as a House of Formation for Adult Catholics, Sherry Weddell. Siena Institute Press.

the **called** *&* **gifted** *workshop*   Administration

Administration

empowers a Christian to be an effective channel of God's wisdom by providing the planning and coordination needed to accomplish good things.

■ **Scripture and Catechism references**

Genesis 39:2–6; 41:46–49, 53–57
Acts 6:1–7
I Corinthians 12:28
Exodus 18:17–23
Romans 12:7
CCC 898–900; 907; 909–911

■ **Recommended books**[†]

Life of St. Dominic, Augusta Theodosia Drane. Tan Books.

The Life and Wisdom of Margaret of Scotland, Lavinia Byrne. Alba House. Saints Alive Series.

The Making of a Christian Leader, Ted Engstrom. Zondervan Publishing.

The 7 Habits of Highly Effective People, Stephen Covey. Simon & Schuster.

Principle-Centered Leadership, Stephen Covey. Fireside.

Faith-Based Management: Leading Organizations That Are Based on More Than Just Mission, Peter C. Brinckerhoff. Wiley Nonprofit Law, Finance and Management Series.

Collaboration: Uniting Our Gifts In Ministry, Loughlan Sofield, and Carroll Julian. Ave Maria Press.

The Collaborative Leader: Listening to the Wisdom of God's People, Loughlan Sofield, Donald H. Kuhn, and Delores Leckey. Ave Maria Press.

■ **Some possible expressions**

executive	office manager/administrative assistant
parish administrator	parish council /board member
homemaker	administrative/finance council
commmittee head	community or parish organizer

Patron saints for the charism of Administration

■ Saint Pulcheria (399–454)

Pulcheria was co-ruler of the Byzantine Empire with her brother at the age of fifteen. She was well-educated, multilingual, a devout Christian, and exceptionally competent in affairs of state. She founded the University of Constantinople, developed a code of law, and worked for peace and the welfare of her people through lower taxation.

■ Saint Margaret of Scotland (1045–1093)

An English girl who married the illiterate warrior King of Scotland, Margaret was happy in her marriage and a gifted administrator who was enormously influential for good in her adopted country. Margaret reformed the law courts in the favor of the poor, ransomed slaves, forbade royal soldiers to loot Scottish homes, founded churches, and organized church synods. Her eight children were all known for their faith and virtue.

■ Saint Dominic (1170–1221)

Dominic Guzman founded his famous order of preaching friars (the Dominicans) as a response to the crisis of a wide-spread heretical movement in France known as Albigensianism. Dominic's evangelistic zeal was complemented by his formidable organizational abilities. Dominic organized his order on democratic lines at a time when this was unheard of and ensured that each friar had the freedom necessary to respond effectively to the needs about him. The original thirteenth century rule was so well suited to the order's preaching mission that it has remained largely unchanged for nearly eight hundred years.

■ Saint Vincent de Paul (1580–1660)

The catalyst of a widespread spiritual revival in seventeenth century France, Vincent organized an order of priests to serve as missionaries to the poor in the countryside, reformed the training of priests and, with Saint Louise de Marillac, founded the Sisters of Charity. Vincent was a brilliant administrator whose organizational abilities enabled him to create a nation-wide charitable network that cared for the needs of the sick, the poor, orphans, the aged and galley slaves. The Society of Saint Vincent de Paul was founded in the nineteenth century by eight lay students led by Frederic Ozanam, who was beatified in 1997.

■ Venerable Pauline Marie Jaricot (1799–1862)

A gifted administrator, Pauline organized a brilliant method for collecting money for missionary work (now known as the Society for the Propagation of the Faith) and also founded the Association of the Living Rosary. Her remarkable success aroused jealousy. When the funds for one of her projects were embezzled by a trusted advisor, many of Pauline's supporters turned against her and she spent the rest of her life trying to pay the donors back. She was friends with the famous Saint John Vianney, the Curé d'Ars.

Celibacy

empowers a Christian to be most fulfilled and spiritually fruitful by remaining unmarried and celibate for the sake of Christ.

■ **Scripture and Catechism references**

Matthew 19:11–12
I Corinthians 7:7–9, 32–35
CCC 915–916; 922–924; 1579–1580; 1832; 2231–2233; 2337–2359

■ **Recommended books[†]**

Kateri Takakwitha, Lillian M. Fisher. Pauline Books.

Philip Neri: The Fire of Joy, Paul Turks & Daniel Utrecht. Alba House.

Virginity: A Positive Approach to Celibacy for the Sake of the Kingdom of Heaven, Raniero Cantalamessa, O.F.M., Cap. Alba House.

Celibacy, Prayer and Friendship: A Making-Sense-Out-of-Life Approach, Christopher Riesling. Alba House.

And You are Christ's: the Charism of Virginity and the Celibate Life by Thomas Dubay, S.M. Ignatius Press.

■ **Some possible expressions**

(Celibacy is always used in conjunction with other gifts and frees a person for total dedication to any work or calling.)

priesthood
religious sister or brother
lay missionary worker
work withthe poor
ministry to single adults

[†]Many of these titles are available through the Siena Institute website, www.siena.org.

Patron saints for the charism of Celibacy

■ Saint Isabella of France (1225–1270)

Daughter of the King of France and sister to Saint Louis IX, the devout and well-educated Isabella became seriously ill. A renowned holy woman brought to her sickbed prophesied that Isabella would recover her health but remain dead to the world. Despite several offers of marriage from politically important suitors, Isabella convinced her family and a skeptical Pope that she should be allowed to remain a virgin for life. Isabella founded a convent (which she did not enter); led a life of prayer, mortification, and service to the poor and sick; and died as a laywoman at forty-five.

■ Saint Philip Neri (1515–1595)

Philip Neri, as famous for his jokes as for his ability to read souls, played a central role in the sixteenth-century evangelization of the city of Rome. Philip lived contentedly as a single layman until the age of thirty-five, befriending and evangelizing the young men of Rome, caring for poor pilgrims, and founding a hospital for the poor. Philip became a priest at the insistence of his spiritual director and eventually founded the Congregation of the Oratory, which provided informal spiritual exercises for laymen. Many of his personal disciples entered religious life and became powerful influences for good in the life of the Church and the city of Rome.

■ Blessed Kateri Tekakwitha (1656–1680)

Kateri was a Mohawk Indian who lived in upstate New York during the first century of European colonization. She was baptized by Jesuit missionaries and withstood serious persecution from her tribe for becoming a Christian, finally escaping to a Christian Indian village. Greatly impressed by the example of French nuns, Kateri desired to take a vow of perpetual virginity and finally convinced her Jesuit spiritual director to let her do so, even though taking such a vow was unheard of among her own people. Kateri lived as a consecrated laywoman until her death at age twenty-four.

Craftsmanship

empowers a Christian to be an effective channel of God's goodness to others through artistic or creative work that beautifies and/or orders the physical world.

■ Scripture and Catechism references

Exodus 28:2–5; 31:1–11
Sirach (Ecclesiasticus) 38:27–34
Acts 18:3
CCC 337–339; 341; 349; 2415; 2427–2428; 2500–2503; 2513

■ Recommended books[†]

General works about the Christian understanding of creation and creativity:
  The Mind of the Maker, Dorothy Sayers. Harper San Francisco.
  Only the Lover Sings, Josef Pieper. Ignatius Press.
  The Beauty of Holiness and the Holiness of Beauty: Art, Sanctity, and the Truth of Catholicism, John Saward (features the paintings of Fra Angelico). Ignatius Press.
  Towards a Theology of Beauty, John Navone. Liturgical Press

Biography and works of individuals:
  Fra Angelico (Colour Library), Angelico, Christopher Lloyd, and David White. Phaidon Press.
  Proud Donkey of Schaerbeek : Ade Bethune, Catholic Worker Artist, Judith Stoughton. North Star Press.

Icons:
  The Icon: Window on the Kingdom, Michel Quenot. St. Vladimir's Seminary Press.
  The Art of the Icon: A Theology of Beauty, Paul Eydokimov. Oakwood Publications.

[†]Many of these titles are available through the Siena Institute website, www.siena.org.

Homemaking:
>*The Hidden Art of Homemaking,* Edith Schaeffer. Tyndale House.

Gardening:
>*Catholic Traditions in the Garden,* Ann Ball. *Our Sunday Visitor.*
>*Monastic Gardens* by Michael Hales, Mick Hales. Steward, Talbori & Chang.

Cooking:
>*A Continual Feast: A Cookbook to Celebrate the Joys of Family and Faith Throughout the Christian Year,* Evelyn Birge Vitz. Ignatius Press.
>*Cooking With The Saints: An Illustrated Treasury of Authentic Recipes Old and Modern,* Ernst Schuegraf. Ignatius Press.

Architecture:
>*Architecture in Communion,* Steven J. Schloeder. Ignatius Press.
>*Architecture of Silence: Cistercian Abbeys of France,* David Heald (Photographer), Terryl Nancy Kinder (Introduction), Harry N. Abrahms.

■ Some possible expressions

artist or artisan	creative homemaker
cook	handyman
calligrapher or illustrator	interior designer or architect
clothing designer	landscape designer or gardener
icon painter	woodworker

Patron saints for the charism of Craftsmanship

■ Saint Joseph

Husband of the Virgin Mary and foster-father of Jesus, Joseph was a carpenter by trade and was known as a "just man." He is patron of the Universal Church and of workers, and he was a great favorite of Saint Teresa of Avila, who named the first convent of Discalced Carmelites in his honor.

■ Saint Bridgit of Ireland (c. 453)

One of the most famous women in Irish history, Bridgit was the daughter of a pagan Irish chieftain and a female Christian slave. Known for her great generosity and independence of mind, Bridgit chose to live as a consecrated virgin, praying and making vestments and tapestries for churches. She founded the first religious houses for women in Ireland, some of which became great centers of art and literature. Although Mother Abbess of thousands, she was most often found at the end of her life milking cows and tending sheep.

■ Blessed John of Fiesole (Fra Angelico) (1386–1455)

One of the greatest fresco painters of the middle ages, this Dominican friar was known as "Friar Angel" because, as one contemporary put it, "no one could paint like that without first having been to heaven." His motto was "to paint Christ, one must live Christ."

■ Blessed James Duckett (d. 1602)

James lived in England and converted to Catholicism during a time of terrible persecution. He made his living by printing and dealing in Catholic books. He was arrested so often for this daring activity that he spent nine out of his twelve years of married life in prison. Betrayed by a fellow Catholic and sentenced to death for binding a book of Catholic apologetics, James was driven to his execution in the same cart as his accuser, whom he publicly forgave.

■ Ade Bethune (1914-2002)

Ade Bethune was a 19-year-old artist when she first met Dorothy Day. Ade created many famous woodcuts of worker saints and the corporal works of mercy for the Catholic Worker newspaper. She took in poor young women as apprentices into her home and trained them in both the fine arts and the arts of living. Ade brought the same creative intensity to cooking and gardening as to sculpture, painting, crafting mosaics, carving wood, and liturgical art. Dorothy Day said of Ade: "Whenever I visited Ade, I came away with a renewed zest for life. She has such a sense of the sacramentality of life, the goodness of things."

Discernment of Spirits

empowers a Christian to be an effective channel of God's wisdom by accurately perceiving a divine or demonic presence in certain people, places or things.

■ Scripture and Catechism references

Matthew 16:21–23
Acts 16:16–18
I Corinthians 12:10
I John 4:1–6
CCC 391–395; 397–398; 407–411; 539; 550; 1082–1083; 1237; 1668–1673; 1706–1709; 2115–2117; 2850–2854

■ Recommended books[†]

John of the Cross: Doctor of Light and Love, Kieran Kavanaugh. Crossroads.

A Still, Small Voice: A Practical Guide on Reported Revelations, Fr. Benedict Groeschel. Ignatius Press.

Resist the Devil: A Pastoral Guide to Deliverance Prayer, Charles Harris. Greenlawn Press.

Deliverance from Evil Spirits: A Practical Manual, Francis MacNutt. Chosen Books.

■ Some possible expressions

spiritual direction
counseling
healing ministry
intercessory prayer
leadership

[†]Many of these titles are available through the Siena Institute website, www.siena.org.

Patron saint for the charism of Discernment of Spirits

■ **Saint John of the Cross (1542–1591)**

Born into poverty in Spain, John became one of the first two male members of the reformed Carmelite order started by Saint Teresa of Avila. During his lifetime, John was often called upon to discern the spiritual experiences of others and is today recognized as one of the foremost authorities on mystical experience in Christian history. In his writings, he deals at length with the many forms that spiritual deception can take.

Encouragement

empowers a Christian to be an effective channel of God's love—nurturing others through his or her presence and words of comfort, encouragement, and counsel.

■ Scripture and Catechism references

Acts 4:36; 14:19–22; 15:30–32; 20:1–2
Romans 12:8
I Corinthians 12:8, 9
I Thessalonians 2:11–12
I Thessalonians 5:9–11
Hebrews 3:13; 10:24, 25
II Peter 3:15, 16
CCC 1749–1845; 2447

■ Recommended books†

A Rocking-Horse Catholic, Caryll Houselander. Sheed & Ward.

Doctor of the Heart: An Autobiograhy, Conrad W. Baars. Alba House.

Healing the Unaffirmed: Recognizing Deprivation Neurosis, Conrad W. Baars & Anna A. Terruwe. Alba House.

Healing as a Parish Ministry, Leo Thomas and Jan Alkire. Ave Maria Press.

Healing Ministry: A Practical Guide, Leo Thomas and Jan Alkire. Sheed and Ward.

Holy Listening: The Art of Spiritual Direction, Margaret Guenther. Cowley Publications.

The Art of Christian Listening, Thomas N. Hart. Paulist Press.

†Many of these titles are available through the Siena Institute website, www.siena.org.

Encouragement

■ Some possible expressions

- counseling
- spiritual direction
- mentoring
- parenting
- small group facilitator
- teaching (especially children)
- prayer team
- grief ministry
- evangelism
- eucharistic minister to the sick
- helping professional

Patron saints for the charism of Encouragement

■ Saint Barnabas

First mentioned in Acts 4, Barnabus was a Jewish Christian from Cyprus named Joseph, who was nicknamed by the apostles "Barnabas," which meant "the Son of Encouragement." A generous man, he sought to reconcile Saint Paul and John Mark (Acts 15). Barnabas was recognized during his lifetime as both a prophet and an apostle and accompanied Paul on some of his missionary journeys.

■ Saint Francis De Sales (1567–1622)

One of the most lovable of men, Frances de Sales was a remarkably successful evangelist in the Savoy region of France and was made bishop of the very people he had brought back into the Church. Famous for his gentleness and patience, Francis was a gifted writer and a remarkable spiritual friend and director. He enjoyed a close and loving friendship with Saint Jeanne de Chantal with whom he founded the Visitation Sisters.

■ Caryll Houselander (1901-1954)

A very popular English devotional writer, Caryll Houselander was sometimes called the "Divine Eccentric" by her friends and admirers. She was a reclusive, chain-smoking mystic who wore startling dead white make-up, possessed a wicked sense of humor, and had an intense vision of the suffering Christ. Caryll carried on a vast correspondence with hundreds of people all over the world. She had extraordinary success in counseling deeply troubled children who had been traumatized by their experiences of the war. As an admiring psychiatrist put it, "she loved them back to life."

■ Conrad Baars (1919-1981)

Conrad Baars was born and raised in Holland. He became a medical student, fled Holland after the Nazis conquered it, and joined the French resistance. Conrad was captured by the Germans and sent to the Buchenwald concentration camp. By the time he was liberated after 19 months of terrible suffering, Conrad was clear that only God gives life meaning. After the war, Baars immigrated to the US and became a psychiatrist. Together with Dr. Anna Terruwe, he developed a new psychological method based on the psychology of St. Thomas Aquinas that took seriously the spiritual dimension of human beings and involved the healing of the whole person.

Evangelism

empowers a Christian to be an effective channel of God's love by sharing the faith with others in a way that draws them to become disciples of Jesus and responsible members of his Church.

■ Scripture and Catechism references

Acts 5:27–32, 42; 11:20–21; 14:21
Romans 10:14, 15
II Corinthians 4:1–7
Ephesians 4:11–13
I Thessalonians 1:4–6; 2:13
II Timothy 4:1–5
CCC 27–49; 74–79; 150–166; 169–171; 425–429; 604–605; 613–618; 767–768; 836–856; 904–905; 1256–1261; 1814–1816; 2442

■ Recommended books[†]

Philip Neri: The Fire of Joy, Paul Turks. Alba House.

Catherine of Siena: A Biography, Anne B. Baldwin. *Our Sunday Visitor.*

The Living of Maisie Ward by Dana Greene, University of Notre Dame Press.

Evangelizing Unchurched Children: A Pocketbook for Catechists, Therese Boucher. Resource Publications.

The Ministry of Evangelization, Susan W. Blum. The Liturgical Press.

In the Power of the Spirit: Effective Catholic Evangelism, Kevin Ranaghan. Resurrection Press.

News That is Good: Evangelization for Catholics, Robert J. Hater. Ave Maria Press.

John Paul II and the New Evangelization, Ralph Martin and Peter Williamson. Ignatius Press.

[†]Many of these titles are available through the Siena Institute website, www.siena.org.

Some possible expressions

religious education
RCIA/returning Catholics programs
apologetics
lector
religious writing
lifestyle or friendship evangelism
missionary
political, social, or cultural change agent

Patron saints for the charism of Evangelism

Saint Catherine of Siena (1347–1380)

Catherine was a single woman and a lay Dominican. After three years of solitude and prayer as a teenager, she re-entered the world with a sense of personal mission. Many were converted after only a few minutes in her presence, and she kept three Dominican priests busy hearing the confessions of her penitents. Catherine was often called in to arbitrate feuds, counseled heads of state, convinced Pope Gregory XI to return to Rome from Avignon, and worked ceaselessly for the healing of schism in the Church. Catherine is the only layperson who has been declared a Doctor of the Church.

Saint Francis Xavier (1506–1552)

Converted by Saint Ignatius of Loyola, Francis ranks as one of the greatest evangelists in Christian history. He left Europe for India on twenty-four hours' notice and in the next ten years founded Catholic communities in parts of south India, Malaysia, Indonesia, and Japan. In one letter, Francis estimated that he had baptized ten thousand new Christians in one month and admitted that there were days when he was so exhausted from the continual baptisms that he could no longer lift his hands. Francis died on a tiny island six miles off the coast of China preparing to bring the Christian faith to that immense nation.

Patron saints continued ⇨

Evangelism

■ Saint Marguerite Bourgeoys (1620–1700)

Born in France, Marguerite was asked to be part of a lay-initiated venture to found a colony at Quebec for the sake of evangelizing the Iroquois Indians of Canada. Carrying only a tiny bundle of clothing and disregarding the very real risk of martyrdom, Marguerite sailed to Quebec where she constantly evangelized sailors, soldiers, and children despite terrific obstacles. She eventually founded the Congregation of Notre Dame, an order of sisters dedicated to the teaching and evangelization of young women.

■ Saint Joseph Moscati (1880–1927)

A layman and brilliant physician, he was well-known for his heroic efforts to save his patients during a cholera epidemic and an eruption of Mount Vesuvius. Joseph was convinced that the health of the body was dependent upon the state of the soul and he regularly encouraged his patients to draw nearer to God and return to the sacraments. He gave free medical care to the poor, the homeless, and religious and had a gift for diagnosis that seemed to his colleagues to border on the miraculous.

■ Frank Sheed (1897-1982) & Maisie Ward (1889-1975)

This husband and wife team of apologist-evangelist and writer helped fire a 20th century Catholic literary renaissance. Frank was raised in an anti-Catholic Protestant family in Australia, converted to Catholicism as a teenager, and immigrated to England as a young lawyer. Maisie was born into a wealthy, upper-crust, intensely Catholic English family. Frank and Maisie met while promoting street-corner apologetics for the Catholic Evidence Guild. Both Frank and Maisie continued street preaching well into the 1950's. In addition to their own books, their firm of Sheed & Ward published the works of the greatest Catholic writers and apologists of their day including G. K. Chesterton, Ronald Knox, Dorothy Day, and Evelyn Waugh.

Faith

empowers a Christian to be an effective agent of God's purposes through an unusual trust in the love, power, and provision of God and a remarkable freedom to act on this trust.

■ Scripture and Catechism references

Luke 7:1–10; 17:5–6
Acts 27:21–25
Romans 4:18–21
I Corinthians 12:9
II Corinthians 4:13–14, 16–18; 5:7
Hebrews 11
CCC 144–184; 222–227; 814–1816

■ Recommended books and videos[†]

Mother Teresa, Ann and Jeanette Petrie (video). Ignatius Press.

St. Francis of Assisi: A Biography, Omer Englebert. Servant Publications.

Immigrant Saint: The Life of Mother Cabrini, Pietro Di Donato. St. Martin's Press.

Mother Cabrini: Missionary to the World, Frances Parkinson Keyes. Ignatius Press.

The Life of Saint Teresa of Avila by Herself, J.M. Cohen (Translator). Penguin Classics.

■ Some possible expressions

exceptionally generous giver	fund-raising
entrepreneur	founder
innovator	visionary
intercessory prayer	healing prayer team
parenting	
leader of cutting edge organization or group	

[†]Many of these titles are available through the Siena Institute website, www.siena.org.

Patron saints for the charism of Faith

■ Saint Teresa of Avila (1515–1582)

Mystic, reformer of the Carmelite order, and Doctor of the Church, Teresa was a woman of unstoppable faith. She started the discalced (shoeless) Carmelite order in the teeth of ferocious opposition. All of her reformed Carmelite houses were founded in great poverty and dependent upon alms. When Teresa heard that the dreaded Spanish Inquisition was examining her writings for heresy, she laughed, as Teresa was fond of saying: "Why should we not expect great things of God? We serve One who is all powerful."

■ Saint Frances Xavier Cabrini (1850–1917)

Frances longed to be a missionary from childhood and Pope Leo XIII sent her to the Americas. She and the members of her order (Missionary Sisters of the Sacred Heart) started hospitals, schools, orphanages, and ministries to immigrants and prisoners. Whenever things looked particularly impossible, Frances always took it as a sure sign that God was about to do something wonderful. Once bandits fired at her at close range, but the bullet dropped harmlessly to her side. Frances wasn't surprised—hadn't she commended herself to the protection of the Sacred Heart of Jesus?

■ Saint Maximilian Mary Kolbe (1894–1941)

Born in Poland, Maximilian was only thirteen when he joined the Franciscan order. A man of contagious vision, he founded the Militia of Mary Immaculate and published millions of copies of the Militia bulletin in several languages. Maximilian also founded the "City of the Immaculate," a self-sustaining town made up of hundreds of friars dedicated to evangelization through the modern media. Arrested by the Nazis for assisting Jews, he was sent to Auschwitz where he died because he voluntarily offered to take the place of another in the dreaded starvation bunker.

Giving

empowers a Christian to be a cheerful channel of God's provision by giving with exceptional generosity to those in need.

■ Scripture and Catechism references

Malachi 3:10
Matthew 25:34–45
Mark 12:41–44
Luke 6:30
Acts 4:34–36; 11:28–30
Romans 12:8
II Corinthians 8:1–15
Galatians 5:22–23
CCC 1434; 1438; 1832; 1969; 2437–2463

■ Recommended books and videos[†]

Mother Teresa, Ann and Jeanette Petrie (video). Ignatius Press.

Margaret, Friend of Orphans, Mary Lou Widmer, Pelican Publishing Co.

St. Katherine Drexel: Friend of the Oppressed, Ellen Terry. Pauline Books.

Generous Living: Finding Contentment through Giving, Ron Blue and Jodie Berndt. Zondervan Publishing.

Gifts From the Heart: Giving to God What Belongs to God, Larry Burkett. Northfield Publishing.

Giving and Stewardship in an Effective Church: A Guide for Every Member, Kennon Callahan. Jossey-Bass Publishing.

Stewardship: A Disciple's Response, U.S. Catholic Conference of Bishops pastoral letter.

†Many of these titles are available through the Siena Institute website, www.siena.org.

Giving

■ Some possible expressions

fund-raising
board member of charitable organization
exceptionally generous giver
philanthropist
financial expert
creative worker for social/economic justice
hospitality

Patron saints for the charism of Giving

■ Saint Melania the Younger (d. 439)

A member of the Roman nobility, Melania convinced her mother and husband to abandon their luxurious lifestyle and become part of a Christian community of thirty families. Against family opposition, she sold her vast properties and gave the money to the needy while purchasing the freedom of eight thousand slaves. Melania knew Saint Augustine, founded double monasteries for her former slaves, and finally settled in Jerusalem close to Saint Jerome.

■ Saint Homobonus (d. 1197)

The heir to a successful mercantile business, Homobonus (which means "good man" in Latin) looked upon his trade as opportunity given to him by God. He was hard working, successful, and happily married. Not content with merely tithing, Homobonus was remarkably generous, seeking out the poor in their homes and caring for them. Devoted to the Blessed Sacrament, Homobonus died while kneeling in prayer during Mass.

■ Saint Katherine Drexel (1858–1955)

As a teenager in a fabulously wealthy and devout family, Katherine had a vision of the Blessed Virgin Mary who told her "Freely you have received, freely give." Katherine shared her dream of founding schools for Native and African Americans with the Pope who encouraged her to start a missionary order that that purpose. She was known as the "richest nun in the world" because of the great wealth at her disposal to give away. Katherine died at 97 and left behind six hundred sisters and sixty-one schools for Native and African Americans.

■ Blessed Bartolo Longo (1841–1926)

Bartolo's incredible saga began when he was "ordained" as a Satanic priest during his university days in Naples. Brought back to the Christian faith by the witness of a friend, he became a vigorous advocate of the Rosary and built a magnificent church in Pompeii dedicated to the Virgin of the Rosary. A respected lawyer, Bartolo and his wife spent much of their time and income caring for many orphans and paid for the training of forty-five seminarians.

■ Margaret Haughery (1814-1882)

Margaret was born in Ireland but lived most of her life in New Orleans. She lost everyone she loved—parents, husband, and infant daughter—by the time she was 22. Although she was illiterate, Margaret was an exceptionally gifted businesswoman who dedicated her life to making money in order to help the poor. Working with Catholic sisters to care for the orphans of New Orleans, this uneducated emigrant began to show a completely unsuspected talent for raising and making money. She started first by begging for money and food and later founded the first steam bakery in the entire south. A devout Catholic, she lived a life of great simplicity and became known as the "mother of orphans" because she gave vast sums to support the orphans of the city. Greatly loved, seated in the doorway of her famous bakery she was consulted for her business wisdom by the rich and the poor. She was known simply by all in New Orleans as "our Margaret," and when she died, the entire city mourned for her.

Healing

empowers a Christian to be a channel of God's love through whom God cures illness and restores health when healing is unlikely to occur quickly or to happen at all.

■ Scripture and Catechism references

II Kings 5:9–16
Tobit 11:1–19
I Corinthians 12:9, 28
James 5:14–16

Sirach (Ecclesiasticus) 38:1–15
Luke 9:1–6
Acts 3:1–10; 5:12–16; 9:32–35
CCC 517; 547–549; 1499–1523

■ Recommended books[†]

Healing, Francis MacNutt. Ave Maria Press.

The Power to Heal, Francis MacNutt. Ave Maria Press.

Healing as a Parish Ministry, Leo Thomas and Jan Alkire. Ave Maria Press.

Healing Ministry: A Practical Guide, Leo Thomas and Jan Alkire. Sheed and Ward.

Saint Julie Billiart: The Smiling Saint, Mary Kathleen Glavich. Pauline Books.

Set All Afire: A Novel About Saint Francis Xavier, Louis De Wohl. Ignatius Press.

St. Martin De Porres: Apostle of Charity (Cross and Crown Series of Spirituality), Giuliana Cavallini, Caroline Holland (Translator). Tan Books.

Father Solanus: The Story of Solanus Casey, O.F.M., Cap., Catherine Odell. Our Sunday Visitor.

Nothing Short of a Miracle: The Healing Power of the Saints, Patricia Treece. *Our Sunday Visitor.*

[†]Many of these titles are available through the Siena Institute website, www.siena.org.

Some possible expressions

healing prayer minister
medical professional
counseling
intercessory prayer
helping professional

eucharistic minister to the sick
caregiver
spiritual direction
pastoral staff

Patron saints for the charism of Healing

Saint Francis Xavier (1506–1552)

Converted by Saint Ignatius of Loyola, Francis is probably the greatest missionary in Christian history. He founded Catholic communities in parts of south India, Malaysia, Indonesia, and Japan. Francis's gift of healing was an important component of his evangelistic success. On one occasion, there is evidence that Francis raised a young man from the dead. In India, he was in such demand to pray over the sick that he finally sent out some of the newly baptized Indian children to pray over the sick in his place—and many were healed.

Saint Philip Neri (1515–1595)

Philip Neri, as famous for his jokes as for his ability to read souls, played a central role in the sixteenth century evangelization of the city of Rome. While praying in the catacombs, Philip experienced a burning globe falling out of the sky into his mouth and entering his heart, which seemed to expand and burn with love. Philip often held the sick and sorrowful to his great, quivering heart and they were mysteriously quieted and healed. After his death, an autopsy showed that his two of his ribs were broken in order to accommodate his abnormally large heart.

Patron saints continued ⇨

Healing

■ Blessed Anna Maria Taigi (1769–1857)

Anna was the poor wife of a rough and temperamental Roman porter. For forty-seven years, she was granted something unique in the history of saints, the continuous vision of a luminous disc in which she could see present and future events anywhere in the world. In addition, Anna had a wonderful gift of healing. Many were healed by the application of oil from a little lamp that always burned before a small statue of the Virgin Mary in Anna's house. Others were healed through her touch or the sign of the cross.

■ Saint Julie Billiart (1751–1816)

Paralyzed for twenty-three years, Julie accepted her illness cheerfully and still managed to hide priests in her house during the French Revolution. Julie had a vision of Christ surrounded by an order of sisters dedicated to teaching and trusted that someday she would be healed and the vision would come to pass. At fifty-two, she started a small religious house and after a Novena to the Sacred Heart of Jesus was dramatically healed. Julie also received the gift of healing and once healed twenty of her sisters laid low by typhoid fever.

■ Saint Martin de Porres (1579–1639)

St. Martin de Porres began life as the illegitimate son of a Spanish officer and a free black woman in Peru. He was apprenticed to a physician as a child and entered the Dominican Order as a lay brother at 15. Martin was a skilled physician with a reputation as a healer and miracle worker. The sick and poor flocked to him and many remarkable healings were attributed to him during his lifetime. He is revered as the patron saint of interracial justice.

Helps

empowers a Christian to be a channel of God's goodness by using his or her talents and charisms to enable other individuals to serve God and people more effectively.

■ Scripture and Catechism references

Exodus 18:13–27
Mark 15:40–41
Romans 16:1–2
I Corinthians 12:28
I Peter 4:10–11
CCC 907; 910; 1143

■ Some possible roles

administrative assistant/secretary	support staff
volunteer	ghost writer/editor
mentor	pastoral staff
teaching	parenting
spiritual direction	

Patron saints for the charism of Helps

■ Saint Macrina (fourth century)

The daughter of two saints (Basil and Emmelia), Macrina was well-educated and the eldest of ten children. When her fiancé died suddenly, Macrina decided to devote herself to the education of her younger siblings. She had a tremendous influence on three of her brothers who became saints and fathers of the Church (Saints Gregory of Nyssa, Basil the Great, and Peter of Sebastea). Gregory of Nyssa wrote that it was from his sister Macrina that he and his brothers learned humility, prayer, and love of the Scriptures.

■ Saint Paula (347–404)

A Roman noblewomen and widow, Paula became the great friend, disciple, and assistant of Saint Jerome. Paula was part of a group of devout women that gathered around Jerome in Rome and accompanied him into exile in Bethlehem. Paula knew Greek, taught herself Hebrew, and helped Jerome in both his scholarly work and his disputes. She founded several monasteries, had her daughters and granddaughter educated by Jerome, and is buried under the altar of the Church of the Nativity in Bethlehem, the traditional birthplace of Jesus.

■ Brother Leo (flourished 1209–1244)

One of the first companions of Saint Francis of Assisi, Leo was ordained and served as Francis' confessor and secretary. From 1220, Leo was Francis' constant companion and nursed him in his last illness. Leo was with Francis when he received the stigmata. Francis had a great love for Leo and spoke of him as the ideal friar. We only possess two letters in Francis' own handwriting—one is a letter to Leo and the other is a blessing for Leo that includes the beautiful "Praises of God."

■ Saint Anne Line (1569–1601)

Living during the terrible persecution of Catholics in sixteenth-century England, Anne was raised as a Calvinist, openly converted to the Catholic faith during her teens, and was disowned by her family. She was happily married, but her Catholic husband was arrested and forced into exile for attending Mass. When a secret refuge was created for priests in London, Anne was asked to manage the guest house. Government agents raided Anne's home and found an altar decorated for Mass. She was convicted of the then-capital crime of aiding a Catholic priest and was executed by hanging for her faithfulness.

Called & gifted workshop

Hospitality

empowers a Christian to be a generous channel of God's love by warmly welcoming and caring for those in need of food, shelter, and friendship.

■ Scripture and Catechism references

Genesis 18:1–8
Matthew 25:34–45
Acts 16:14, 15
Galatians 4:14
I Peter 4:9
CCC 1832; 2446–2449; 2463

II Kings 4:8–17
Luke 17:19–31; 24:28–31
Romans 12:13
Hebrews 13:1–2
III John 5–8

■ Recommended books†

Biographies:

St. Benedict: Hero of the Hills, Mary Fabyan Windeatt. Ignatius Press

The Long Loneliness, Dorothy Day. Harper.

Guides to personal hospitality:

A House of Many Blessings: A Christian Guide to Hospitality, Quin Sherrer and Laura Watson. Vine Books.

The Gift of Hospitality: In Church, in the Home, in All of Life, Delia Halverson. Chalice Press.

A Continual Feast: A Cookbook to Celebrate the Joys of Family and Faith Throughout the Christian Year, Evelyn Vitz. Ignatius Press.

The Welcoming Hearth, Elizabeth Skoglund. Tyndale House.

Guides to community hospitality:

Making Room: Recovering Hospitality As a Christian Tradition, Christine D. Pohl. Eerdmans.

Ministry of Hospitality, Sylvia Cirone Deck. Sheed and Ward.

Entertaining Angels: Hospitality Programs for the Caring Church, Elizabeth Rankin Geitz. Morehouse Publishing.

Hospitality

the called & gifted workshop

■ Recommended books† (continued)

Welcome! Tools & Techniques for New Member Ministry, Andrew Weeks. Alban Institute.

■ Some possible expressions

hospitality	industry
hospitality committee/usher	organizing conferences/retreats
refugee resettlement	work with homeless/poor
small Christian communities	RCIA/returning Catholics program
hospitality in your home	receptionist

Patron saints for the charism of Hospitality

■ Saint Benedict (c. 547)

The founder of western monasticism, Benedict left Rome as a teenager to live a solitary life given to prayer. Wherever he went, disciples were drawn to him by his sanctity and miraculous powers. Benedict organized these disciples into communities, especially at Monte Cassino, now the most famous monastery in the world. Many came to visit and seek Benedict's counsel and all were welcomed and housed. Hospitality is a very important part of Benedictine life to this day, and every guest is to be received as though he were Jesus.

■ Saint Margaret Clitherow (1556–1586)

An English butcher's wife, Margaret converted to Catholicism at eighteen. She was imprisoned several times for practicing her faith. Margaret had a secret room constructed in her home where priests and liturgical gear could be hidden, and her house became an illegal "Mass center." A foster child gave away the location of the secret room after being threatened, and Margaret was arrested. She refused to plead in order to prevent her children from being forced to testify against her and was executed by being pressed to death.

■ Saint Swithin Wells (1536–1591)

Swithin was a Catholic teacher during the years of persecution in England. With his wife, he reconciled many to the Catholic faith and opened his home as a refuge for priests, who came at all hours of the day. Swithin also rented rooms in which catechetical instruction could be given. Government agents broke into his house while Mass was being said and arrested everyone present. Swithin was hung, drawn, and quartered. Mrs. Wells, after being forced to watch her husband's execution, spent the rest of her life in prison.

■ Dorothy Day (1897–1980)

Orthodox in her faith and radical in her politics, Dorothy was one of the most remarkable women of the twentieth century. A journalist and committed Communist, Dorothy entered the Catholic church after the birth of her only child. Possessed of a great love for the Catholic faith, Dorothy founded the Catholic Worker Movement, which still offers personal, sacrificial hospitality to the homeless and abandoned while passionately advocating social justice and opposing war. Cardinal O'Connor of New York has begun the cause of Dorothy's canonization.

Intercessory Prayer

empowers the intense prayer of a Christian for others to be the means by which God's love and deliverance reaches those in need.

■ Scripture & Catechism references

Genesis 18:20–32
II Maccabees 12:39–45
Acts 12:5–17
II Corinthians 1:8–11
Colossians 4:12–13
I Timothy 2:1–3
James 5:14–16
CCC 968–970; 2626–2649; 2683; 2850–2865

■ Recommended books

Life of St. Dominic, Augusta Theodosia Drane. Tan Books.

Story of a Soul: The Autobiography of Saint Therese of Lisieux, Institute of Carmelite Studies.

To Quell the Terror: The Mystery of the Vocation of the Sixteen Carmelites of Compiègne, Guillotined July 17, 1794, William Bush. Institute of Carmelite Studies.

Intercession: A Guide to Effective Prayer, Sr. Ann Shields. Servant Publications.

Pray and Never Lose Heart: The Power of Intercession, Sr. Ann Shields. Servant Publications.

A Rachel Rosary: Intercessory Prayer for Victims of Post Abortion Syndrome, Larry Kupferman. Resurrection Press.

Prayer of the Faithful: Understanding and Creatively Leading Corporate Intercessory Prayer, Walter Costner Huffman.

The Peacemaking Power of Prayer: Equipping Christians to Transform the World, John D. Robb & Jim Hill. Broadman & Holman.

Some possible expressions

>group intercession
>personal intercessor for leader
>healing prayer team
>prayer chain or prayer group
>prayer walking
>counseling
>spiritual direction
>RCIA
>returning Catholics team
>leader
>parent
>community activist

Patron saints for the charism of Intercessory Prayer

Saint Dominic (1170–1221)

Dominic Guzman founded his famous order of preaching friars (the Dominicans) as a response to the crisis of a widespread heretical movement in France. Dominic was a powerful intercessor. When a brilliant young man about to join the order, Reginald of Orleans, fell desperately ill, Dominic turned to prayer. Reginald was granted a vision of the Blessed Virgin Mary through which he was instantly healed. Dominic sought to spend his days talking to people about God and his nights talking to God about the needs of people.

The Carmelite Nuns of Compiègne (d. 1794)

In September 1792, France was in the midst of revolution. A small Carmelite community of nineteen nuns began to daily offer their lives as a holocaust to God "so that peace might be restored to the church and the state." By 1793, Robespierre's Reign of Terror was underway and anyone suspected of opposing the government was sent to the guillotine. The Carmelites of Compiègne were all arrested in July 1794, condemned for their "fanaticism," and guillotined on July 17, 1794. Ten days later, Robespierre fell from power and the Terror ended.

■ Saint Thérèse of Lisieux (1873–1897)

Thérèse sought to join the Discalced Carmelite nuns at the age of fifteen. When she was refused admission because of her age, Thérèse boldly asked the permission of the Pope during a public audience. Finally permitted to join in 1888, Thérèse was a fervent intercessor for priests and for missionary work. She died of tuberculosis at twenty-four, and her spiritual autobiography, *The Story of a Soul,* has made her one of the most popular of saints. Thérèse, the cloistered intercessor, has been named patroness of all foreign missions.

Knowledge

empowers a Christian to be a channel of God's truth through diligent study and intellectual activity that enables us to better understand God, ourselves, and the universe.

■ Scripture and Catechism references

Proverbs 2:1–11
Wisdom 7:16–22
Sirach (Ecclesiasticus) 38:3, 6
II Corinthians 11:6
Colossians 2:2–3
CCC 31–49; 84–133; 156–171; 184; 1949–1986

■ Recommended books[†]

The Dumb Ox: Saint Thomas Aquinas, G. K. Chesterton. Image Books.

The King's Good Servant but God's First: The Life and Writings of Saint Thomas More, James Monti. Ignatius Press.

Edith Stein: St. Teresa Benedicta of the Cross, Maria Ruiz Scaperlanda, Susanne M. Batzdorff, Michael Linssen. Our Sunday Visitor.

Raissa Maritain: Pilgrim, Poet, Exile, Judith D. Suther. Fordham UP.

John Henry Newman: His Life and Work, Brian Martin. Continuum Publishing Group.

Scientist and Catholic: Pierre Maurice Marie Duhem, Stanley Jaki. Christendom Press.

The Idea of a University, John Henry Newman. Regnery Publications.

Hooked on Philosophy: Thomas Aquinas Made Easy, Robert O' Donnell (also deals with the philosophy of Gilson, Maritain, and John Paul II). Alba House.

Creation and Scientific Creativity: A Study in the Thought of Stanley Jaki, Haffner. Christendom Press.

[†]Many of these titles are available through the Siena Institute website, www.siena.org.

Knowledge   *the* **called** *&* **gifted** *workshop*

■ Some possible expressions

    teaching　　　　　　　　　　preaching
    scholarship　　　　　　　　　　philosophy
    technology and science　　　　　educational conferences, retreats
    apologetics　　　　　　　　　　writing
    home schooling　　　　　　　　RCIA, religious education, parish council
    leadership (especially of educational or high tech organizations)

Patron saints for the charism of Knowledge

■ Saint Thomas Aquinas (1225–1274)

When at nineteen years old Thomas first joined the Dominican order, his horrified family locked him up in a castle for two years before relenting. Thomas studied under Saint Albert the Great and was widely recognized as one of the greatest scholars of his day. He lectured at the University of Paris and in Italy and wrote several books, including the famous *Summa Theologiae*. In 1272, Thomas received a revelation from God that affected him so much, he stopped writing altogether. Thomas has been named universal Doctor of the Church and has exercised a profound influence on the Church to this day.

■ Saint Thomas More (1478–1535)

Thomas More was one of those gifted beings who had it all. A successful lawyer and member of Parliament, an internationally famous scholar and writer, and a favorite of the King of England, More was adored by his children and renowned for his wit. His friend Erasmus wrote, "He seems to have been born to make jokes." But nothing was as important to More as his Catholic faith. Thomas refused to take an oath recognizing the King as supreme head of the Church in England, was convicted of treason, and was beheaded in the Tower of London.

■ Venerable John Henry Newman (1801–1890)

Raised as an evangelical Anglican, young Newman met Oxford scholars who were rediscovering Church tradition. Newman and his friends caused national turmoil by advocating that the Anglican church cease to be Protestant and adapt a "middle way" between Protestantism and Roman

Catholicism. Newman's historical findings convinced him to enter the Catholic Church in 1845. A brilliant intellectual and writer, Newman has been hugely influential. His ideas permeated the Second Vatican Council, which has been called the "Council of Newman."

■ Saint Edith Stein (1891–1942)

Born into a devout Jewish family in Germany, Edith Stein sought the truth in philosophy. She earned her Ph.D. in philosophy and was an assistant to the famous Edmund Husserl. In 1921, she read Teresa of Avila's autobiography, instantly recognized "this is the truth", and became a Catholic. When Hitler came to power in Germany, Edith entered a Carmelite monastery to pray for her people and their persecutors while continuing to write scholarly works. In 1942, Edith and her sister Rosa were taken to Auschwitz where they died in a gas chamber.

■ Saint Niels Steensen (Nicholas Steno) 1638-1686)

This remarkable Danish man was both a ground-breaking scientist and a convert-bishop in his relatively short life. Steensen was recognized as a brilliant young scientist and discovered, among other things, the circulation of blood in the human body. He is also considered to be the founder of the science of geology. After wrestling with doubts about the Lutheran faith, he became a Catholic at age 29. He later became a priest and a missionary bishop to northern Germany, where he gave everything he had to the poor and died at a young age, worn out by his apostolic labors.

■ Blessed Frederic Ozanam (1813-1853)

Challenged to "show us your works" by anti-Christian skeptics at the University of Parish, 20-year-old Frederick Ozanam and seven friends started the first St. Vincent de Paul conference, personally visiting the poor in their homes and meeting their needs. As a professor at the Sorbonne, he was convinced that the Gospel had renewed or revivified all the good to be found in the ancient European cultures and sought to communicate this vision through his scholarly works. He enjoyed a very happy marriage and was devoted to his wife and daughter. He faced death at the young age of 40 with great faith and serenity and was declared Blessed in 1997.

Leadership

empowers a Christian to be an agent of God's purposes by sharing a compelling vision of a better future with others and by directing the overall efforts of a group as they work together to make the vision a reality.

■ **Scripture and Catechism references**

I Samuel 10:1
II Chronicles 1:7–12
Nehemiah 2:17–18
Daniel 10:3
Mark 9:33–35
Acts 1:5–26; 6:1–6
Romans 12:8
Hebrews 13:17
CCC   763–771; 874–896; 897–900; 903; 907–913; 1878–1885; 1897–1948; 2442

■ **Recommended books[†]**

Forget Not Love: The Passion of Maximilian Kolbe, André Frossard. Ignatius.

St. Ignatius of Loyola: The Pilgrim Years, James Brodrick, SJ. Ignatius Press

Mary Ward, Sister Margaret Mary. Continuum Publishing Group.

The Life of Saint Teresa of Avila by Herself, J.M. Cohen (Translator). Penguin Classics.

Konrad Adenauer: The Father of the New Germany, Charles Williams, et al. John Wiley & Sons.

Setting Hearts on Fire: A Spirituality for Leaders, Timothy Brown and Patricia Sullivan. Alba House.

Who's in Charge? Leadership Skills for Clergy and Others in Ministry, James Harvey. Loyola Press.

The Making of a Christian Leader, Ted Engstrom. Zondervan Publishing.

Leaders: The Strategies for Taking Charge, Warren Bennis & Burt Nanus. Harper & Row.

[†]Many of these titles are available through the Siena Institute website, www.siena.org.

the **called** *&* **gifted** *workshop* | Leadership

■ Recommended books[†] (continued)

Principle-Centered Leadership: Strategies for Personal and Professional Effectiveness, Stephen R. Covey. Simon and Schuster.

The Making of a Leader: Recognizing the Stages of Leadership Development, J. Robert Clinton. Navpress.

■ Some possible expressions

pastor of large parish	leader of community activities
innovator	small group leader
teaching/preaching	family life
head of organization/group/business	
chairperson of any board/committee	
founder of new movement/organization/group	

Patron saints for the charism of Leadership

■ Saint Ignatius of Loyola (1491–1556)

Born in Spain, Ignatius' military career was cut short by a canon ball at age thirty-one. While confined to bed, he was converted by reading the lives of the saints. Ignatius eventually gathered a group of disciples who agreed to take a vow of going wherever the Pope should send them for the salvation of souls. He was fifty when he became the first superior general of the Society of Jesus (the Jesuits). A wonderful organizer and judge of men, Ignatius spent the rest of his life in Rome directing the complex affairs of this far-flung order.

■ Saint Teresa of Avila (1515–1582)

Mystic, reformer of the Carmelite order, and Doctor of the Church, Teresa was a woman of tremendous vision and courage. She started the discalced (shoeless) Carmelite order in the teeth of ferocious opposition. Witty and charming, she personally founded sixteen women's houses and facilitated the founding of a discalced men's order with the assistance of a wide circle of clerical and lay supporters. As Teresa was fond of saying, "Why should we not expect great things of God? We serve One who is all powerful."

■ Mary Ward (1585–1645)

Born into a family of English Catholics who endured great persecution, Mary started a non-enclosed teaching order for women (based on the Jesuit model) to help win England back to the Catholic faith. A champion of women's education and their apostolic capacities, Mary endured much hardship and opposition. Her order was temporarily banned and she was briefly suspected of heresy and imprisoned, only to be released by a Papal order. Resilient and courageous, Mary once observed that in difficult times "cheerfulness is next to godliness."

■ Saint Madeleine Sophie Barat (1779–1865)

Madeleine's older brother discerned that his sister was called to a special vocation and gave her the kind of education usually reserved at that time for boys going into the priesthood. All Catholic schools in France were destroyed during the Revolution, so Madeleine's brother asked her to found an order of sisters dedicated to the education of girls. Madeleine's leadership gift was so marked that she was made superior of the order at the age of twenty-three and retained the office for sixty-three years.

■ Saint Maximilian Mary Kolbe (1894–1941)

Born in Poland, Maximilian was only thirteen when he joined the Franciscan order. A man of contagious vision, he founded the Militia of Mary Immaculate and published millions of copies of the Militia bulletin in several languages. Maximilian also founded the "City of the Immaculate," a self-sustaining town made up of hundreds of friars dedicated to evangelization through the modern media. Arrested by the Nazis for assisting Jews, he was sent to Auschwitz where he died because he voluntarily offered to take the place of another in the dreaded starvation bunker.

the **called** *& gifted workshop*

Mercy

empowers a Christian to be a channel of God's love through practical deeds of compassion that relieve the distress of those who suffer and help them experience God's love.

■ Scripture and Catechism references

Sirach (Ecclesiasticus) 38:1–15
Isaiah 58:5–10
Micah 6:8
Matthew 20:29–34; 25:34–45
Mark 9:41
Luke 10:30–37
John 8:3–11
Acts 11:28–30
Romans 12:8
CCC 864; 899; 1807; 1822–1829; 1849; 2437–2463

■ Recommended books and videos[†]

They Called Her the Baroness: The Life of Catherine de Hueck Doherty, Leone Hanley Duquin. Alba House.

Leper Priest of Moloka'i: The Father Damien Story, Richard Stewart. University of Hawaii Press.

Mother Teresa, Katheryne Spink (the complete authorized biography updated to include Mother Teresa's death). Harper Collins.

Mother Teresa, Ann and Jeanette Petrie (video). Ignatius Press.

Love: A Fruit Always in Season, Dorothy S. Hunt, editor (daily Meditations by Mother Teresa). Ignatius Press.

Heart of Joy: The Transforming Power of Self-Giving, Mother Teresa. Servant Publications.

Spiritual Journeys: An Anthology by People Working with those on the Margins, Sr. Stanislaw Kennedy, R.C.S., editor (includes pieces by Jean Vanier and Henri Nouwen). Ignatius Press.

Some possible expressions

medical professional	social work
prison ministry	eucharistic minister to the sick
pastoral work	work with the poor or homeless
social justice activist	missionary
volunteer chore services	voluntary poverty

Patron saints for the charism of Mercy

Henrietta Delille (1813–1862)

Henrietta was born in New Orleans into a free family of mixed race whose daughters were raised to be elegant mistresses of wealthy white men. She first became aware of the possibility of another kind of life for a woman when, at the age of fourteen, she began helping a French nun teach the catechism to slaves. In the face of many legal and social barriers, including the opposition of her own family, Henrietta founded an order of African-American nuns who identified with and ministered to slaves and the black community, educating children and caring for the poor, the sick, and orphans.

Saint Joseph Moscati (1880–1927)

A layman and brilliant physician, he was well-known for his heroic efforts to save his patients during a cholera epidemic and an eruption of Mount Vesuvius. Joseph was convinced that the health of the body was dependent upon the state of the soul, and he regularly encouraged his patients to draw nearer to God and return to the sacraments. He gave free medical care to the poor, the homeless, and religious and had a gift for diagnosis that seemed to his colleagues to border on the miraculous.

Catherine de Hueck Doherty (1896-1984)

Born into a upper-class family in Russia, Catherine survived revolution, starvation, war, and a compulsively unfaithful first husband. After converting to Catholicism and emigrating to Canada, she lived with the poor and worked for racial and economic justice. Catherine's first marriage was eventually annulled. Eddie Doherty, a famous American journalist, gave up all his possessions in order to marry her. Forced out of organizations that she had founded in Toronto and New York, she started all over again at the age of 51 in Combermere, Ontario. There she founded Madonna House and wrote spiritual works that combined the insights of Western and Eastern Christianity.

■ Blessed Damien of Molokai (1840-1888)

The most famous Catholic of his generation was born in Belgium and was sent as a missionary to Hawaii where he was ordained a priest in 1865. At his own request, Fr. Damien was sent to the dreaded leper colony of Molokai in 1873. In addition to his normal duties as a priest, he nursed lepers with his own hands, buried the dead, and designed and built numerous churches, dormitories, and other buildings for the residents of the island. In 1885, it became clear that Fr. Damien had contracted leprosy himself, but he continued his heroic service until his death in 1888. He was declared Blessed in 1994.

■ Blessed Teresa of Calcutta (1910-1997)

Born into a devout Catholic family in Albania, Agnes Gonxha Bojaxhiu entered the Irish Sisters of Loretto at 18 where she was given the name Teresa. She was sent to Calcutta, India, in 1929 where she served as a school teacher for many years. While on retreat in September of 1946, Teresa received a "call within a call" to work among the poorest of the poor. In 1950, she founded the Missionaries of Charity, dedicated entirely to whole-hearted and free service to the poorest of the poor. By the time she died in 1997, Teresa was the most revered woman in the world and had received many honors, including the Nobel Peace Prize. Her date of Beatification is October 19, 2003.

Missionary

empowers a Christian to be a channel of God's goodness to others by effectively and joyfully using his or her charisms in a second culture.

■ **Scripture and Catechism references**

Matthew 28:16–20
Acts 8:4, 5, 26–39; 9:10–19; 10:25–28; 14:26–28; 17:19–31
Romans 10:14–15
I Corinthians 9:19–23
CCC 763–768; 774–782; 836–856; 931; 1256–1261; 1275–1284

■ **Recommended books†**

Set All Afire: A Novel of St. Francis Xavier, Louis de Wohl. Ignatius Press.

Immigrant Saint: The Life of Mother Cabrini, Pietro Di Donato. St. Martin's Press.

Mother Cabrini: Missionary to the World, Frances Parkinson Keyes. Ignatius Press.

Your Mission, Should You Accept It: An Introduction for World Christians, Stephen Gaukroger. Intervarsity Press.

Working Your Way to the Nations: A Guide to Effective Tent-Making, Jonathan Lewis, editor. Intervarsity Press.

■ **Some possible expressions**

missionary/lay volunteer
work with foreign students/refugees/immigrants
work with racial/cultural/linguistic minority groups
inner city work
racial justice

†Many of these titles are available through the Siena Institute website, www.siena.org.

Some possible expressions, continued

> reconciliation/peace-making
> pastoral work
> teaching
> preaching
> evangelism
> social justice activist

Patron saints for the charism of Missionary

Blessed Raymond Lull (1232–1316)

> Educated as a knight, Raymond underwent a conversion at thirty-one. Dedicating himself to winning Muslims to Christ, Raymond learned Arabic. He wrote major works of theology in Latin, Catalan, and Arabic. Raymond helped to found Franciscan monasteries in which friars could be prepared for missionary work in the Muslim world. He made two unsuccessful missionary trips to North Africa himself, but the traditional story of his martyrdom there does not seem to be historically based.

Saint Francis Xavier (1506–1552)

> Converted by Saint Ignatius of Loyola, Francis may be the greatest missionary in Christian history. He left Europe for India on twenty-four hours notice and in the next ten years founded Catholic communities in parts of south India, Malaysia, Indonesia, and Japan. Reporting in one of his letters, Francis estimated that he had baptized ten thousand new Christians in one month. He died on a tiny island six miles off the coast of China while preparing to bring the Christian faith to that immense nation. He is the patron saint of foreign missions.

Patron saints continued ⇨

■ Saint John de Britto (1647–1693)

The favorite companion of the heir to the throne of Portugal, John fought his way into the Jesuit order at fifteen. After ordination, John spent the rest of his life working in southeast India under circumstances of incredible difficulty. He adapted himself completely to the lifestyle, food, language, and customs of the local people. Many Indians responded to his ministry and became Catholics even in the face of torture and violence. John was beheaded by an Indian prince in 1693.

■ Saint Frances Xavier Cabrini (1850–1917)

Frances longed to follow her namesake Francis Xavier to China, but Pope Leo XIII sent her to the Americas. She started hospitals, schools, and orphanages and ministered to immigrants and prisoners throughout North and South America. Whenever things looked particularly impossible, Frances took it as a sure signthat God was about to do something wonderful. After her death, reports of 150,000 miracles flooded the Vatican. Frances is the patron saint of immigrants.

■ Venerable Edel Quinn (1907-1944)

Edel was a 20-year-old typist in Dublin when she was introduced to the Legion of Mary, an international lay organizationfor door-to-door evangelism and works of mercy. Edel longed to become a nun but was refused because she was diagnosed with tuberculosis. When Edel had recovered, the Legion decided to send this frail woman to Africa to start evangelistic groups of lay people. Cheerful, eager, and fearless, no difficulties were too much for Edel to tackle. After a remarkably successful ministry, her health gave way and she died at 37. Edel's beatification is expected soon.

Music

empowers a Christian to be a channel of God's creative goodness to others through writing or performing music for the delight of others and the praise of God.

■ Scripture and Catechism references

Exodus 15:1, 2
I Samuel 16:14–23
I Chronicles 16:41–42
II Chronicles 5:12–14; 29:25–30
Psalm 150
Ephesians 5:19–20
James 5:13
CCC 1136–1144; 1156–1158; 1177; 1191; 2500–2503; 2513

■ Recommended books[†]

Hildegard of Bingen, 1098-1179: A Visionary Life, Sabina Flanagan. Routledge.

Hungry for Heaven: Rock 'n Roll and the Search for Redemption, Steve Turner. Intervarsity Press.

Reflections on the Spirituality of Gregorian Chant, Dom Jacques Hourlier. Paraclete Press.

Music Education in the Christian Home, Mary Froechlich. Noble Publishing.

Only the Lover Sings, Josef Pieper. Ignatius Press.

Best and Brightest Stories of Hymns, Fr. George Rutler. Ignatius Press.

Te Deum: The Church and Music, Paul Westermeyer. Fortress Press.

[†]Many of these titles are available through the Siena Institute website, www.siena.org.

Music   *the* **called** *&* **gifted** *workshop*

■ Some possible expressions

> choral/instrumental performance
> professional musician
> music therapy/music education
> media work
> worship/music ministry in a parish/prayer group
> composing/arranging
> directing musical groups
> entertaining family and friends

Patron saints for the charism of Music

■ Blessed Hildegard of Bingen (1098–1179)

> Raised by Blessed Jutta, a hermitess, Hildegard became a nun at fifteen and prioress of her community at thirty-eight. She received many visions which were submitted to the Pope, who approved her prophecies and their publication. Hildegard had many gifts, one of which was music. She wrote both the words and music to many hymns and anthems for her community. At the end of her life, she wrote a long letter about sacred music which, as she put it, "helps man to build a bridge of holiness between this world and the World of all Beauty and Music."

■ Giovanni Pierfuigi da Palestrina (1525–1594)

> Known by the name of his hometown, Palestrina lived in Rome with his wife. There he was a disciple of Saint Philip Neri, whose influence helped him gain spiritual insight into the Mass and express it through music. He worked with Saint Charles Borremeo to implement the liturgical reforms of the council of Trent. As a composer of music for the Mass, Palestrina has no peer. His music is still loved and performed in St. Peter's basilica and all over the world, and he is recognized as the greatest musical voice of the Catholic Reformation.

Pastoring

empowers a Christian to be an effective channel of God's love and build Christian community by nurturing the relationships and long-term spiritual growth of a group.

■ Scripture and Catechism references

Ezekiel 34:1–16
John 10:1–16
Acts 20:28
Ephesians 4:11–16
I Thessalonians 2:6–12
I Timothy 3:1–13
I Peter 5:1–4
CCC 900; 902; 910–911; 1546–1548; 1551; 1558–1560; 1585–1586; 1588; 1655–1658; 2447

■ Recommended books[†]

The Parish: Mission or Maintenance?, Michael Sweeney, OP and Sherry Weddell. Siena Institute Press.

The Making of a Pastoral Person, Rev. Gerald R. Niklas. Alba House.

Building Community: Christian, Caring, Vital, Loughlan Sofield, Rosine Hammett, and Carroll Juliano. Ave Maria Press.

Parish! The Pulitzer Prize-Winning Story of a Vibrant Catholic Community, Robert F. Keiler. Crossroads Publishing.

From Holy Hour to Happy Hour: How to Build Christian Community, Francis X. Gaeta. Resurrection Press.

Excellent Catholic Parishes: The Guide to Best Places and Practices, Paul Wilkes. Paulist Press.

†Many of these titles are available through the Siena Institute website, www.siena.org.

Some possible expressions

priesthood
leader of small faith-centered organization or group
pastoral staff
prayer group leader
Bible study leader
facilitator of small Christian community
parenting
teacher

Patron saints for the charism of pastoring

Saint Charles Borremeo (1538–1584)

A nephew of Pope Pius IV, Charles masterminded the third and final session of the Council of Trent and drew up the Catechism of Trent. Charles was made a bishop in 1563 and left Rome for his diocese in Milan. There he became legendary as he worked to implement the reforms of Trent, to ensure the teaching of the faith, and to care for poor and sick. He miraculously survived an assassination attempt by a renegade priest who was angered by his reforms. Charles is revered to this day as a model of dedicated pastoral care.

Catherine Sanzo (d. 1655)

The wife of a poor Chinese workman, Catherine was already a grandmother when she first heard a Dominican missionary preach and was convinced of the truth of the Catholic faith. Christians were undergoing great persecution in China at this time, but Catherine was undismayed. Recognizing her gifts, the missionaries sent her on catechetical journeys to other villages where she organized Christian discussion and study groups. Catherine also brought back to the faith a number of apostate Christians who had been frightened away by persecution.

■ Blessed Henry the Shoemaker (d. 1666)

Born to a working class family in Luxembourg, Henry combined the trade of shoemaker with a deep spiritual life. Henry prayed and fasted for the spiritual welfare of his fellow shoemakers and formed a religious association for shoemakers. The members had prayer in common, attended daily Mass, visited prisons and hospitals, and made an annual retreat. Association branches started up in other cities, and other tradesmen started similar groups. Henry's biography was entitled, *The Christian Artisan, or the Life of Good Henry.*

■ Blessed Josefa Naval Gerbes (1820–1893)

A Spanish laywoman whose education was limited to reading and embroidery, Josefa was nevertheless well-informed about the Catholic faith. She came up with an imaginative way to share the faith with others: free embroidery lessons accompanied by spiritual reading. Her house became a center of religious formation for young women. The curriculum included basic catechesis as well as instruction in prayer and practical preparation for both marriage and religious life.

Prophecy

empowers a Christian to be a channel of divine truth and wisdom by communicating a word or call of God to individuals or a group through inspired words or actions.

Scripture and Catechism references

Luke 3:1–18
Acts 11:27–30; 15:30–35; 21:9–14
Romans 12:6
I Corinthians 12:10, 28; 14:1–5, 24–30, 37–40
Ephesians 4:11–16
CCC 61; 64; 218; 36; 711–715; 783; 785; 2447

■ Recommended books†

Elijah Task, John Sanford. Victory House.

Prophecy: Exercising the Prophetic Gifts of the Spirit in the Church, Bruce Yocum. Servant Books.

■ Some possible expressions

prayer group
charismatic Mass
intercession
healing prayer teams
counseling
spiritual direction
social justice activist/ministry
teaching/preaching
writing
influential religious/spiritual figure
leader of counter-cultural group/organization

†Many of these titles are available through the Siena Institute website, www.siena.org.

Patron saints for the charism of Prophecy

■ Agabus (first century)

Mentioned in Acts 11:28 and 21:10 as a prophet, Christian tradition holds that Agabus was one of the seventy-two disciples (Luke 10:1) and one of the martyrs who suffered at Antioch. According to Acts 11:27–30, Agabus predicted a famine, which apparently must be identified with that happening in the fourth year of Claudius, 45 A.D. In the year 58, the prophet predicted to St. Paul his coming captivity, though Agabus could not convince the apostle to stay away from Jerusalem (Acts 21:10–11).

■ Saint Philip Neri (1515–1595)

Philip Neri, as famous for his jokes as for his ability to read souls, played a central role in the sixteenth century evangelization of the city of Rome. Philip's prophetic gift was so well-known to his friends that if they were talking and the conversation started to take a wrong turn, they would stop themselves, certain that Philip would know what they had been discussing. Frederick Borremeo, brother of Saint Charles Borremeo, told many stories of Philip's prophetic ability to know, even at a distance, the trials of his spiritual sons and daughters.

■ Blessed Anna Maria Taigi (1769–1857)

Anna was the poor wife of a rough and temperamental Roman porter. For forty-seven years, she was granted something unique in the history of saints: the continuous vision of a luminous disc in which she could see present and future events anywhere in the world. She was consulted by Popes, religious, and civic leaders and many members of the nobility, but she would always leave her exalted guests to greet her husband upon his return home.

Patron saints continued ⇨

■ Dorothy Day (1897–1980)

Orthodox in faith and radical in politics, Dorothy was one of the most remarkable women of the twentieth century. A feminist and committed Communist before her conversion, Dorothy entered the Catholic Church after the birth of her only child. She sought to live the faith without compromise, founded the Catholic Worker Movement, and took vigorous, prophetic stands regarding racism, economic justice, and opposition to war. Dorothy often quoted Dostoyevsky's *Brothers Karamazov:* "Love in practice is a harsh and dreadful thing compared to love in dreams."

the **called** *&* **gifted** *workshop*   Service

Service

empowers a Christian to be a channel of God's purposes by recognizing the gaps or unmet needs that prevent good things from happening and by personally doing whatever it takes to bridge the gap or meet the need.

■ Scripture and Catechism references

Luke 22:24–27
John 13:3–5, 12–17
Acts 6:1–7
Romans 12:7
I Corinthians 16:15–16
CCC 601; 713; 786; 898–899; 903; 909–911; 1937; 2447

■ Recommended books[†]

Improving Your Serve, Charles Swindoll. Word Books.

Friend of the Soul: A Benedictine Spirituality of Work, Norvene Vest. Cowley Publications.

■ Some possible expressions

exceptional volunteer	community/parish activist
handyman or woman	support staff
administrative assistant	service worker
troubleshooter	ombudsman
critical committee member	eager implementer
homemaker	

[†]Many of these titles are available through the Siena Institute website, www.siena.org.

Patron saints for the charism of Service

■ Sir John Burke (d. 1610)

The son of an Irish baron, John ran an ingenious underground for Catholic priests in a time of persecution. In 1608, John's castle was surrounded and attacked while Mass was being celebrated. John and his friends spirited the priests out a back way, but one priest was caught. John rescued the priest then successfully fought his way through the English soldiers and disappeared into his own underground. In 1610, John was betrayed, arrested, and condemned. In his final speech, he commended all that he had, an unborn child, to the Dominican order.

■ Blessed Catherine Jarrige (1754–1836)

Catherine was born into a peasant farming family in France and became a lay Dominican at twenty-two. Shrewd, fearless, and ingenious, she set up an underground for hunted priests during the French Revolution. Catherine hid them in robber's dens and provided them with food, shelter, safe passage, and false papers. In her region, no babies went unbaptized nor any dying without last rites. The responsibility of the entire religious life of the area rested on her capable shoulders for several years. Catherine also helped restart parish life after the Revolution.

Teaching

empowers a Christian to be a channel of God's truth and wisdom by enabling others to learn information and skills that help them reach their fullest spiritual and personal potential.

■ Scripture and Catechism references

Matthew 28:19–20
Acts 18:24–26; 20:20–21
Romans 12:7
I Corinthians 12:28–31
Ephesians 4:11–14
CCC 425–429; 767–768; 785; 849; 888–892; 900; 903–904; 906; 2447

■ Recommended books[†]

So Favored by Grace: Education in Time of John Baptist De La Salle, Lawrence Colhocker. Christian Brothers Conference.

An Extraordinary Australian: Mary MacKillop: The Authorised Biography, Paul Gardiner.

Mastering Teaching, Earl Palmer, Roberta Hestenes, and Howard Hendricks. Questar Publications.

44 Ways to Expand the Teaching Ministry of Your Church, Lyle E. Schaller. Abingdon Press.

Becoming a Catechist: Ways to Outfox Teenage Skepticism, Willian J. O'Malley. Paulist Press.

The Joy of Being a Catechist: From Watering to Blossoming, Gloria Durka, Ph.D. (Available in Spanish: *La Alegría De Ser Catequista*.)

Catholic Education: Homeward Bound, Kimberly Hahn and Mary Hasson. Ignatius Press.

[†]Many of these titles are available through the Siena Institute website, www.siena.org.

Some possible expressions

> public school/adult education teacher
> religious education/RCIA
> tutoring/volunteer teaching
> creating curriculum
> educational leadership
> home-schooling/parenting
> writing
> apologetics
> counseling/spiritual direction

Patron saints for the charism of Teaching

Saint John Baptist de la Salle (1651–1719)

> John was already ordained when he met a layman who had a vision for starting a school for poor boys. John became involved with the school and finally gathered a nucleus of teachers about him to whom he taught a new way of educating children. This group become the Christian Brothers. To focus entirely on the teaching vocation, John laid down the rule that no brother could become a priest. John's system of education—teaching many children simultaneously and in the vernacular—revolutionized elementary education.

Nano Nagle (1718–1784)

> In eighteenth-century Ireland, Catholic schools were forbidden by the English Protestant government. Nano was from a wealthy family but longed to do something for the poor of Ireland. She secretly opened a school in a slum area. When her family found out, they feared reprisals and cut off her funds, forcing Nano to beg for the money to keep her schools going. Undeterred, Nano also started a lay mission society to follow and catechize the Irish who were forced to emigrate to the West Indies. Nano founded an order of sisters dedicated to educating the poor.

the **called** *&* **gifted** *workshop* Teaching

■ Blessed Mary MacKillop (1842–1909)

Born in Australia, Mary dreamed of becoming a teaching sister. The Church in Australia was tiny and scattered over hundreds of thousands of square miles. Mary thought it was natural that her sisters be free to ride to wherever there was the greatest need rather than be subject to the local bishop. Many women were attracted to the order and Mary's teaching methods, but the order faced great obstacles. At one point, Mary was excommunicated, but the bishop who did this soon repented. Her cause for canonization is now underway.

Voluntary Poverty

empowers a Christian to be a channel of God's loving presence by living a life of cheerful, voluntary simplicity or poverty in order to identify with Jesus and the poor.

■ Scripture and Catechism references

Matthew 5:3; 6:19–33
Luke 9:57–58
Acts 4:34–37
II Corinthians 6:10; 8:9
Philippians 2:5–8
I Timothy 6:6–10
CCC 915; 928–929; 1973–1974; 1986; 2053; 2443–2463; 2544–2557

■ Recommended books[†]

The Lessons of St. Francis: How to Bring Simplicity and Spirituality into Your Daily Life, John Michael Talbot and Steve Rabey. E.P. Dutton.

Freedom of Simplicity, Richard Foster. Harper Mass Market Paperbacks.

Living More With Less, Doris Janzen Longacre. Herald Press.

On Living Simply: The Golden Voice of John Chrysostom, Robert Van de Wayer. Triumph Books.

Simplicity: Finding Order, Freedom, and Fulfillment for Your Life (Reconciling Your Life with Your Values), Ed Dobson. Zondervan Publishing.

■ Some possible expressions

religious sister or brother
member of a third order or lay institute

[†]Many of these titles are available through the Siena Institute website, www.siena.org.

Some possible expressions, continued

- social justice ministry/activist
- missionary
- relief and development worker
- exceptional giver
- contemplative
- prophetic vocation
- intercessory prayer

Patron saints for the charism of Voluntary Poverty

Saint Francis of Assisi (1182–1226)

The most beloved saint in Christian history was the son of a wealthy Italian textile merchant. In 1206, Francis had a vision in which God told him to rebuild his church. When Francis sold some of his father's goods to give the money away, his enraged father disowned him, and Francis renounced all his father's possessions. Three years later, Francis felt called to a life of apostolic poverty and began to preach in the streets. His followers became the Friars Minor (the Franciscans). Francis called "Lady Poverty" his beautiful bride.

Saint Clare of Assisi (1193–1253)

Born into a wealthy family, Clare heard Francis of Assisi preach during Lent and never looked back. On Palm Sunday in 1212, Clare slipped out of her home and ran away to join Francis and his community. Clare became the founder of the Franciscan Second Order or "Poor Clares." She and her community lived a life of absolute poverty, silence, and perpetual abstinence. Clare fought long and hard to have her community's rule reflect strict standards of Franciscan poverty. Clare's rule was approved two days before she died at age sixty.

Wisdom

empowers a Christian to be a channel of God's goodness through remarkable insight that enables him or her to come up with creative solutions to specific problems and make good decisions.

■ Scripture and Catechism references

I Kings 3:5–12
Wisdom chapters 7–10
Acts 6:3, 10
I Corinthians 2:1-16; 12:8
James 1:5, 6
II Peter 3:15
CCC 215–217; 1749–1756; 1776–1802; 1805–1806; 1831; 1835; 1845

■ Recommended books[†]

Margaret, Friend of Orphans, Mary Lou Widmer. Pelican Publishing Co.

Faithful Listening: Discernment in Everyday Life, Joan Mueller. Sheed and Ward.

Weeds Among the Wheat, Discernment: Where Prayer and Action Meet, Thomas H. Green, S.J. Ave Maria Press.

Authenticity: A Biblical Theology of Discernment, Fr. Thomas Dubay, S.M. Ignatius Press.

Clever as Serpents: Business Ethics & Office Politics, Jim Grote and John McGeeney. The Liturgical Press

Seeking Wisdom: Preparing Yourself to Be Mentored, Edna Ellison & Tricia Scribner. New Hope Publishers.

Heaven Begins Within You: Wisdom from the Desert Fathers, Anselm Gruen & Peter Heinegg (Translator). Crossroad/Herder & Herder.

†Many of these titles are available through the Siena Institute website, www.siena.org.

the **called** *&* **gifted** *workshop*   Wisdom

■ **Recommended books, continued**

Wisdom of the Celtic Saints, Edward C. Sellner, Susan McLean-Keeney (Illustrator). Ave Maria Press.

■ **Some possible expressions**

leadership
pastor/pastoral staff
parish council

■ **Some possible expressions, continued**

administration
teaching/preaching
writing
spiritual direction
counseling
helping professions
developing technology
practical innovator
fund-raising
parenting

Patron saints for the charism of Wisdom

■ **Saint John Joseph of the Cross (1654–1734)**

Attracted to the Franciscan friars of the "Alcantarine" reform, John joined them at age sixteen. John was held in such esteem that he was put in charge of a new monastery at twenty and ordained at the unusually early age of twenty-three. He was renowned for his extraordinary insight and wisdom in the confessional. Late in his life, when a dispute between the Spanish and Italian sections of the order threatened to close down the Italian houses altogether, John's wisdom and reputation held the

Patron saints continued ⇨

beleaguered Italian friars together until they could form themselves into a province.

■ Saint Nicholas of Flue (1417–1487)

Happily married and the father of ten children, Nicholas' countrymen appointed him a magistrate and judge because of his integrity and wisdom. At age fifty, Nicholas felt irresistibly drawn to the life of a solitary. With his wife's approval, he left his family. Soon after, he lost all desire for food or drink and ever after observed a perpetual fast. He spent nineteen years as a hermit, his evenings given to the many who called upon him for advice. When Switzerland was on the verge of civil war, Nicholas was consulted and helped the factions come to a unanimous agreement.

■ Caroline Chisholm (1808-1877)

Born in England, Caroline sailed to Australia in 1838 as a young wife and mother, where she was touched by the plight of thousands of poor European immigrants pouring into Australia. Caroline was a devout Catholic and gifted problem-solver who personally found jobs for 11,000 female immigrants who might otherwise have been forced into prostitution.. Riding a white horse, Caroline led caravans of immigrants hundreds of miles into the bush to find new homes. Later, she helped design special immigrant ships which were named after her. Shrewd and fearless, Caroline is widely recognized as one of the great figures in Australian history. For years, her portrait was featured on the Australia five pound note.

†Many of these titles are available through the Siena Institute website, www.siena.org.

the called & gifted workshop — Writing

The charism of Writing

empowers a Christian to be a channel of God's creativity by using words to create works of truth or beauty that reflect the fullness of human experience and bring glory to God.

■ Scripture and Catechism references

Psalms 45:1
Philippians 3:1
I Timothy 3:14–15
I Peter 3:15–16
Jude 3
CCC 898–900; 904–907; 909; 911; 2447; 2464–2513

■ Recommended books†

Sigrid Unset: On Saints and Sinners, Deal Hudson, Ed. Ignatius Press.

Tolkien: Man & Myth, Joseph Pearce. Ignatius Press.

Wisdom & Innocence: A Biography of G.K. Chesterton, Joseph Pearce. Ignatius Press.

Flannery O'Connor: The Woman, the Thinker, the Visionary, Ted R. Spivey. Mercer University Press.

Gerard Manley Hopkins: A Life, Paddy Kitchen. Carcanet Press.

The Mind of the Maker, Dorothy Sayers. Harper, San Francisco.

Walking on Water, Madeleine L'Engle. Harold Shaw Publishing.

Only the Lover Sings, Josef Pieper. Ignatius Press.

■ Some possible expressions

novelist	poet/lyricist
dramatist	journalist
apologist	teacher/preacher
creator of curriculum	public relations/advertising
ghost-writer/editor	speech writer

Patron saints for the charism of Writing

■ Gerard Manley Hopkins (1844–1889)

Hopkins is considered the principal English poet of the nineteenth century, though he published few poems in his lifetime. After corresponding with John Henry Newman, twenty-one-year-old Gerard entered the Catholic Church. He later joined the Jesuits and gave up writing. In 1875, at the request of his superiors, he began writing again and composed the famous "Wreck of the Deutschland" in honor of five Franciscan nuns drowned in a shipwreck. Hopkins' poems often express a sense of the glorious presence of God in and through creation.

■ Gilbert Keith Chesterton (1874–1936)

A popular English journalist, G. K. Chesterton was a huge man famous for his joyful good humor, his wit, and his love of paradox. He was successful in many genres: novels, poetry, biography, and essays. He is best known today for his Father Brown mystery novels. Chesterton was a brilliant Christian apologist while remaining friends with famous skeptics like George Bernard Shaw and H. G. Wells. He was received into the Catholic Church in 1922 and had considerable influence on later Catholic writers like Evelyn Waugh.

■ Sigrid Unset (1882–1949)

Sigrid's father was an archeologist, and she was raised in skeptic and feminist circles. She received the Nobel Prize for Literature in 1928 for her famous trilogy, *Kristin Lavransdattar,* which chronicles the life of a devout and passionate woman in medieval Norway. Sigrid entered the Catholic Church in 1925. Her later writings often have religious themes and express a concern for racial and religious tolerance. An early critic of Nazism, Sigrid fled Norway after the German invasion of 1940 and was unable to return until 1945.

■ Flannery O'Connor (1925–1964)

Flannery is known for her touching and bizarre stories about life in the South. Raised as Catholic in a small town in Georgia, O'Connor moved to New York to write. She was diagnosed with lupus a few years later and returned home to spend the rest of her life in Georgia. Flannery's Catholic faith was deep and well-informed. She once remarked that if the South was not deeply Christian, it was certainly Christ-haunted. Her novels are famous for their grotesque characters and violence, which often mask a deep and abiding faith.

Appendix

The Charism of Public Tongues

empowers a Christian to speak a divinely-anointed message in a language he or she has never learned.

■ Scripture and Catechism references

Acts 2:1–13; 10:44–46; 19:1–7
I Corinthians 12:10, 28; 14:13–19
CCC 799–801; 951; 2003–2005

■ Recommended books[†]

Your Spiritual Gifts Can Help Your Church Grow, C. Peter Wagner. Regal Books.

A Key to Charismatic Renewal in the Catholic Church, Msgr. Vincent Walsh. Key of David Publications.

■ Some possible expressions

prayer groups
"charismatic" masses
intercession
healing prayer teams

the **called** *&* **gifted** *workshop*

The charism of Interpretation of Tongues

empowers a Christian to be a channel of God's truth, direction, or encouragement by making known in the vernacular the contents of a public message or prophecy originally delivered in tongues.

■ Scripture and Catechism references

I Corinthians 12:10, 30; 4: 4–19, 26–28
CCC 797–801; 2003

■ Recommended books[†]

Your Spiritual Gifts Can Help Your Church Grow, C. Peter Wagner. Regal Books.

A Key to Charismatic Renewal in the Catholic Church, Msgr. Vincent Walsh. Key of David Publications.

■ Some possible expressions

prayer groups
intercessory prayer
healing ministry/counseling/spiritual direction

the **called** *&* **gifted** *workshop*